A Child's First Library of Learning

Feelings & Manners

TIME-LIFE BOOKS • ALEXANDRIA, VIRGINIA

Contents

Do Manners Matter? 4

Why Shouldn't I Talk When My Mouth Is Full? 6

Why Should I Cover My Mouth When I Cough or Sneeze? 8

Do I Have to Share My Toys? 10

How Should I Act at My Friend's House? 12

May I Cut in Line? 14

What Can I Say When I Meet Someone New? 16

Why Should I Listen to Adults? 18

Why Can't I Use Bad Language? 20

What Is the Point of Saying "Please" and "Thank You"? 22

Why Should I Be Nice to the New Kid? 24

Why Do People Come in All Shapes and Sizes? 26

Why Do Some People Wear Glasses? 28

Why Do Some People Talk with Their Hands? 30

How Old Is Old? 32

Why Do People Have Different Skin Colors? 34

Why Do Some People Talk Funny? 36

Does Everyone Go to Church? 38

Why Are Some People Twins? 40

Why Do People Get Scared? 42

Why Do People Argue? 44

What Should I Do When I Get Mad? 46

How Can I Make New Friends? 48

Why Is Honesty the Best Policy? 50

Why Did I Get Picked Last? 52

Is Keeping a Promise Important? 54

Why Can't I Always Do What My Friends Are Doing? 56

Why Is It Important to Think of Others? 58

What Is "Playing Fair"? 60

Why Is It Bad to Snoop? 62

Is It All Right to Cry? 64

How Can I Help If Something Bad Happens to a Friend? 66

Is It Ever Okay to Be a Tattletale? 68

What's Wrong with Bragging? 70

What Is Loyalty? 72

What Can I Do If People Make Fun of Me? 74

Do People Turn Green with Envy? 76

Why Do I Have to Be Nice to My Kid Sister or Brother? 78

How Can I Help Make the World a Better Place? 80

Growing-Up Album 81

❓ Do Manners Matter?

ANSWER Manners are the way you act when you're around other people. Saying "Please" and waiting for your turn are examples of good manners. Shouting and pushing are bad manners.

Sometimes it's hard to remember to use good manners. Just keep practicing. Your family, your friends, and the people you meet will be happier if you do.

Who is showing good manners in this picture? Who is not?

Yuck!

● **To the Parent**

Children learn good manners from the time they are babies. Lessons in good behavior come from watching adult role models as well as from explicit instructions. Be realistic, though, about what children can learn at different ages. For instance, children under the age of four cannot be expected to share toys willingly. Those under five usually aren't capable of putting themselves in someone else's shoes. At any age, encouragement, consistency, and a flexible attitude are essential when giving lessons in manners.

Why Shouldn't I Talk When My Mouth Is Full?

ANSWER Eating and talking don't go together. If you try to talk when you have food in your mouth, no one will be able to understand what you are saying. Not only that, but most people think it's gross to look at half-eaten food. So chew with your mouth closed, swallow, then talk—between bites.

Shlur-r-r-rp!

What Are Good Table Manners?

Most families have rules about how to act at the dinner table (and the breakfast and lunch table, too). These rules make mealtimes a little more peaceful and pleasant. Good table manners include being polite, staying clean, and taking turns when talking.

◄ Use your napkin
Keep it on your lap to catch falling food. Remember to wipe your hands on your napkin, not on your clothes.

▲ Drink soup without slurping
That "shlurp" noise is not as funny as you think. If the soup is too hot, don't make waves—blow on it gently.

Please pass the bread.

◄ When you can't reach, ask
Even if you're starving, be patient when food is passed around the table. Be ready to pass food that's near you.

► Excuse yourself
When you finish, politely ask if you may leave the table. You may need to clear away your plate, too.

● To the Parent

In many families, mealtime is the only time when everyone sits down together. Table manners set the ground rules for this daily interaction. As always, keep rules age-appropriate. Even toddlers can be taught to wash their hands before eating, to sit straight, and to show a modest amount of discipline at the table.

Why Should I Cover My Mouth When I Cough or Sneeze?

ANSWER When you have a cold, you cough and sneeze a lot. Each time you do, you send a blast of air out of your mouth. Germs can fly out at the same time. If you cover your mouth, it helps keep germs from spreading. The people around you will like that!

■ Un-bear-able coughing

In a crowded place, a cough can disturb the people around you. Look down or away from others—and don't forget to cover your mouth!

8

What Should I Do When Someone Sneezes?

If someone near you sneezes, you don't have to ignore it. You can say "Bless you!" or "God bless you!" Some people say "Gesundheit" instead—that's the German word for "health." If you sneeze and someone says "God bless you!", remember to say "Thank you!"

Bless you!

◄ **Hey, sleepyhead!**
A yawn does not spread as many germs as a cough or a sneeze. Even so, to be polite, you should cover your mouth whenever you yawn.

● **To the Parent**

Most colds are spread by viruses passed hand to hand, but kids are also at risk when a sneeze or cough sends germs airborne. For this reason, the tradition of covering the mouth when sneezing or coughing is both polite and sensible. Children with a cold who remember to cover their mouths should also be reminded to wash their hands with soap and warm water frequently.

9

? Do I Have to Share My Toys?

ANSWER It's fun to play with friends, but sometimes it's difficult, too. Your friends may want to play with your toy—and you may not feel like sharing. But think about it for a minute. If you share your toys, your friends will be happier. They will want to play with you again. In the end, that will make you happier, too.

▲ You don't always have to share. It's okay to keep a special toy—your favorite stuffed animal, for example—to yourself.

■ Hands off my horse!

What happens when people don't share? Sometimes they get into a fight—even if they are friends. Tugging on a toy can break it—oops! Now neither person can play with the toy.

■ Ways to share

▶ **Play together with the toy**
Some toys, like a ball or a board
game, are perfect for sharing.
Have those ready when a friend
comes to visit.

▶ **Try taking turns**
Only one person at a time can
use a toy like a bubble wand,
but everyone can take turns. If
you like, you can set a kitchen
timer to make sure everyone
gets the same amount of time.
Other kids can pop bubbles
while they wait.

◀ **Divvy them up**
Do you have lots of toy
trucks or dolls? Give
every friend one of them
before you start playing.

11

How Should I Act at My Friend's House?

ANSWER A visit to a friend's house can be lots of fun. Many of the rules there will probably be the same ones you have at home. Other rules—about which rooms you can play in, for example, or whether you can watch TV—might be different. Your job as a good guest is to follow the rules of the house and be polite. That way you'll get invited back to play again.

▲ Get a good start
Don't just barge in! Knock politely on the front door, or ring the doorbell. (Don't lean on the doorbell, though—that's annoying.)

▲ Respect the rules of the home
Different people have their own ways of doing things. Try to follow other people's rules when you are in their house. They'll do the same for you.

▼ Wait for your host

When you eat at a friend's house, remember not to start eating until everyone else does, too.

▶ Sample what is served

Don't say "Yuck" or "I don't like this" if your friends serve "strange" food. Try it. Who knows—you might like it! If not, simply say "No thank you" the next time that food is offered.

◀ Do what others do

Watch what your friends do. If your friend cleans up after a meal, help her, even if you don't do that at home.

● To the Parent

Most children grounded in rules of good behavior in their own home have little trouble adapting to the rules at a friend's house. One parent, after hearing a glowing report of her child's behavior at the home of a friend, jokingly remarked, "Children's manners are for export only."

May I Cut in Line?

ANSWER No, you may not cut in line, even though it can be boring to wait. People stand in line for good reasons. A line lets people take turns fairly: Those who come first get to take their turn first. If you cut in line, you are changing the rules. That would not be fair to the people behind you.

■ Line laws

No one likes to wait in line. But you can make it more pleasant for everyone by waiting for the line to move without pushing or shoving. When you get to the front, act quickly so others can take their own turns.

◄ Who's next?

■ Ways of waiting

People don't wait in line at a doctor's office or in a barbershop. They make appointments instead. In a store, they may take slips of paper with numbers on them. That way everyone knows who goes next.

▼ Take a number!

After you!

LIBRARY

■ First isn't always best

A line helps organize things, but you should still think of others. Sometimes it's nice to let someone go ahead of you—especially if that person needs a little extra help!

● To the Parent

For children, the time spent waiting in line—whether at a supermarket or an amusement park—can seem endless. A child's innate sense of fairness can help him or her understand the need to take turns, though. Try distracting a restless child with a verbal game or conversation to make a long line seem to move faster.

What Can I Say When I Meet Someone New?

ANSWER If you are shy—and most people are, sometimes—you might not know what to say to a new person. Even so, you don't want to be impolite or embarrass your family. So when you meet someone new, look him in the eyes and say, "It's nice to meet you." If he holds out a hand, you can shake it when you say hello.

It's nice to meet you!

What Should I Say on the Phone?

Br-r-r-r-ing! Your phone is ringing! Pick it up and say, "Hello." The caller will probably ask to speak to someone in your house—maybe even you! When *you* call someone, try introducing yourself like this: "Hello, this is Andy. May I please speak to Sam?"

■ Telephone rules

If a call is for someone else, say, "Just a minute, please." Then go get that person.

Tell the caller if a person can't come to the phone.

When you take a message, be sure to write it down.

If you dial a wrong number, say, "Excuse me" and hang up.

Don't talk too long. Other people may want to make calls, too!

MINI DATA

■ Handshakes

The history of some manners is surprising. Long ago, people shook hands to show that they were not carrying any weapons. Today, a handshake is still considered a polite way to say hello.

● To the Parent

By the time they are three or four years old, children can learn polite greetings such as "Hello" and "Pleased to meet you." But telephone manners are harder. Start with some basic rules. Remind a child at home alone, for instance, never to reveal that fact to a stranger on the phone. Instead, say that a parent "can't come to the phone right now." Better yet, use a message machine to screen calls.

Why Should I Listen to Adults?

ANSWER Does it seem as though adults are always telling you what to do? That's because grownups such as your parents and teachers care about you. They tell you what to do so that you will stay safe and happy. Think about what might happen if you never listened to them!

Don't forget your coat and lunch!

What Other Adults Should I Listen To?

Some grownups—your teachers, your neighbors, the parents of your friends—know you personally, so they can give you good advice. Other adults, like police officers and firefighters, watch out for all children—and that includes you!

▲ Police

A police officer or crossing guard can help you cross the street. Police and firefighters often visit schools to talk about safety—they're experts!

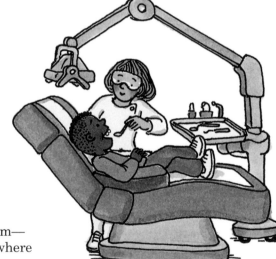

◀ Doctors

Listen carefully to the advice that a dentist or a doctor gives you. They will tell you what you need to do in order to stay healthy.

■ What about strangers?

Don't talk to adults if you don't know them—even if they seem friendly. Never go anywhere with a stranger (rhymes with "danger").

● To the Parent

It may seem obvious to you why children should be polite to adults, but it doesn't hurt to spell it out for the child. At the same time, you'll need to draw the line when it comes to interaction with strangers. You can try acting out some situations with your children to make sure they understand the distinction.

? Why Can't I Use Bad Language?

ANSWER Words have a lot of power. We use them to tell people what we think and feel. Some words, though, are considered "bad," or not polite. People sometimes say them when they get angry or upset. These words can bother the people who hear them. It's better to use other words to tell people how you feel.

Oh, #$^&%@*!!!

■ Think before you blurt

Maybe you know which words are "swear words" and shouldn't be said. But other words can upset people, too. Sometimes the words are not bad, but they hurt someone's feelings. Before you talk about how people look or whether you like them, stop and think: How would you feel if someone said those things about *you?*

What Is the Point of Saying "Please" and "Thank You"?

ANSWER "Please" is a little word that says a lot. It tells people that you need their help. It also tells them that you appreciate what they are about to do for you. Saying "Thank you" to people after they help you lets them know you are grateful for what they did.

May I please go in the water?

Thank you!

▼ **If you please**
"Please" and "Thank you" have been called "magic" words. That's because they almost always make people more willing to help you.

■ Thank-you notes

When someone sends you a gift or does something else especially nice, writing a note is a wonderful way to say thank you.

Dear Aunt Dorothy,
Thank you very much for the, uh,... for your kind gift!

■ Be polite—all over the planet!

Country	"Please"	"Thank you"
Brazil	*Por favor*	*Obrigado*
China	*Qing*	*Xie xie*
Egypt	*Min fadlak*	*Shokran*
France	*S'il vous plait*	*Merci*
Germany	*Bitte*	*Danke*
Israel	*Bevakasha*	*Todah*
Italy	*Per piacere*	*Grazie*
Japan	*Onegai shimasu*	*Arigato*
Kenya	*Asante*	*Tafadhali*
Mexico	*Por favor*	*Gracias*
Namibia	*Asseblief*	*Dankie*
Philippines	*Salamat*	*Paki*

● **To the Parent**

Even toddlers can learn to say "Please" and "Thank you," especially if they hear it frequently at home. Keep in mind, however, that it takes many years for these words to become a habit. Similarly, with a parent on hand to write the message, even a toddler can dictate a thank-you note—but don't despair if you are still reminding your 12-year-old.

? Why Should I Be Nice to the New Kid?

(ANSWER) Can you remember a time when you were in a new place and did not know anyone else? It may have been your first day of school, or perhaps your family had just moved to a new town.

When you were the "new kid" on the block, making friends was extra hard. But if you are an "old kid" on the block, it's easy to be nice. It's also a great way to make new friends.

■ Howdy, neighbor!

When people move to a new house, their toys are packed away, so they can't play with them. Sharing your things with a new neighbor will make him or her feel welcome.

■ Other ways to be nice

▲ **At school**
You can introduce the new kid to some of the people you know. That will help her make new friends.

▲ **After school**
Show the new kid some of your favorite places in the neighborhood. They may soon become *her* favorites, too!

● **To the Parent**

Being "the new kid on the block" is one of childhood's most difficult moments. Children who have settled into familiar friendships may not understand why they should go out of their way to welcome a new arrival. In that case, encourage them to reach out: Help them invite the new kid over to play, and remind them to find out the other child's interests. A new friendship may blossom.

? Why Do People Come in All Shapes and Sizes?

ANSWER Everyone grows differently. Inside you are glands that tell your body how to grow. The pituitary gland controls how tall you will be. Another gland, the thyroid, controls how heavy you will be. You can help your body grow and stay healthy if you remember to eat good food and exercise often.

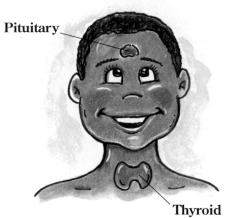

Pituitary

Thyroid

▲ The pituitary gland is in your brain. The butterfly-shaped thyroid gland is in your neck.

■ The three body types

You may be the same size as your friends today, but someday you will all grow to be different sizes. That's because no two bodies grow in exactly the same way. Everyone has a different body type—and a different way of growing up and out.

26

Guess your height and weight

How tall?

As an adult, a typical boy will be about twice as tall as he was at age two. A girl will be about twice as tall as she was at 18 months old.

How heavy?

A grown male weighs five times as much as he did at two. A female weighs five times as much as she did at 18 months.

TRY THIS

Quiet! I'm growing

Measure yourself in the morning, at noon, and at night. You are about ¼ inch taller in the morning than you are at night! Why? Your backbone stretches while you sleep.

CHECK IT OUT

The long and short of it

Robert Wadlow was the tallest man who ever lived. At age eight, he stood 6 feet, 2½ inches tall. By age 22, he was 8 feet, 11 inches tall and weighed 491 pounds! Lucia Zarate, on the other hand, looked like a doll and weighed less than most house cats. As an adult, she was less than 20 inches tall and weighed just 5 pounds.

● To the Parent

"How tall will I be?" and "How fast am I growing?" are questions that children often ask. Marking a height chart on a wall at home will help your child understand how the body grows. It's important for children to feel good about their bodies, no matter what their build. Remind your child that everyone is unique, and that it's what's on the inside that matters.

? Why Do Some People Wear Glasses?

 ANSWER Your eyes are remarkable seeing machines. But they are not always perfect. For some people, the world is a blur. These people have trouble reading books and signs. They may not recognize familiar things. Many people wear glasses or contact lenses so they can see the world better. Glasses and contacts make blurry vision clear again.

▲ In the U.S., one out of every six kids between the ages of 3 and 16 wears glasses or contact lenses.

■ Look! A tank eating peanuts!

Sometimes your eyes fool you. This boy thinks he sees a tank, but his two friends know it isn't a tank at all—it's an elephant! A pair of glasses would help the boy see things the way they really are.

■ Hmm...I need longer arms

This woman is farsighted. To read her newspaper, she must hold it at arm's length. Have you ever seen someone hold a book so close to his eyes that it almost touches his nose? That person is nearsighted. Both people need glasses or contact lenses to see better.

MINI-DATA

■ How far can we see?

The higher up you are, the farther you can see. From the top of a 1,000-foot cliff, for example, you could see for 42 miles.

1000 ft

500 ft

3 ft

2.25 miles   30 miles   42 miles

● **To the Parent**

Most people wear glasses to correct vision problems, which usually result from misshapen eyeballs. Children who express curiosity about eyeglasses should be reminded that people who wear them are not so different from those who do not.

29

❓ Why Do Some People Talk with Their Hands?

ANSWER People who can't hear well often learn to "talk" with their hands. This is called sign language, because they can say as much with hand signs as other people can say with their voices. They can also use the looks on their faces to add meaning to the hand signs.

◄ Here are two hand signs for animal names. The arrows show how to move your hands.

▲ **Elephant**

▲ **Tiger**

■ Sign languages

There are several signing systems for people who can't hear. American Sign Language uses hand movements to stand for words. Another method, the Manual Alphabet *(below),* uses the hands to spell out words letter by letter.

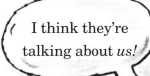

I think they're talking about *us!*

Manual Alphabet

A B C D E F G H I J K L M N O P

Why Do Some People Read with Their Hands?

People who are blind and can't see letters can learn to read patterns of raised dots with their fingertips. The dots form letters in the Braille alphabet (named for Louis Braille, a French teacher of the blind). Books, signs, elevator buttons, and even the names of soft drinks can be printed in Braille.

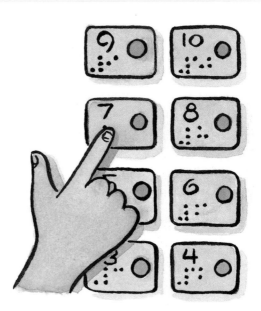

TRY THIS

■ What if you couldn't see?

Find out what it's like to live without sight: Explore your house with your eyes shut or covered with a blindfold. You'll be surprised how much your fingertips can tell you!

● **To the Parent**

Children may be curious, but also dismayed, when they see someone using sign language or vision aids. Matter-of-fact explanations of why these are necessary can help a child relate better to people who look and behave differently. Encouraging children to feel Braille patterns on elevator buttons or to experiment with signing is reassuring as well.

Q R S T U V W X Y Z

❓ How Old Is Old?

ANSWER Anyone who looks grown up may seem old to you. People are called adults when they reach the age of 21. Middle-aged people are those from about 45 to 60 years old. The elderly, or seniors, are older than 65. Many people stay healthy and active into their 80s and 90s.

■ Growing and aging

▲ At 12 months, this girl is exploring her world as she crawls.

▲ At two to four years old, she learns a lot about herself.

▲ From five to 10, most children go to school and make new friends.

▲ Sports and group activities are important for teenagers.

■ We aren't that old!

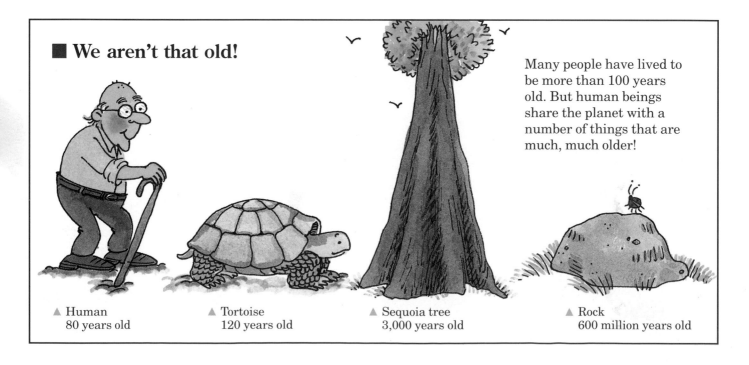

Many people have lived to be more than 100 years old. But human beings share the planet with a number of things that are much, much older!

▲ Human
80 years old

▲ Tortoise
120 years old

▲ Sequoia tree
3,000 years old

▲ Rock
600 million years old

▲ Young adults go to college or train for jobs after high school.

▲ Most grownups take care of jobs and families into their 50s.

▲ People who have retired from work have time to play.

▲ The very old stay active and enjoy their grandchildren.

■ Things seniors do

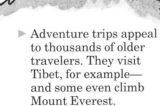

► Adventure trips appeal to thousands of older travelers. They visit Tibet, for example— and some even climb Mount Everest.

▲ Ballroom dancing is popular among seniors. One English couple still dances in contests, even though they are both more than 90 years old.

◄ Weddings aren't for young people only. Many people fall in love and get married after age 65. One groom was 103!

● To the Parent

Grandparents—generous with their time, skills, and attention— are often among the most beloved figures of a child's world. If grandparents are distant or ill, it may be helpful for children to associate with other seniors in order to get a well-balanced picture of normal aging and development.

Why Do People Have Different Skin Colors?

ANSWER Inside your skin is melanin. These tiny brown grains protect your skin from harmful sun rays. People whose ancestors lived where it is very sunny—Australia or Africa, for example—have darker skin, with a lot of melanin. People with ancestors from cloudy countries have lighter skin.

What Is an Albino?

An albino is a person or an animal with no melanin in his skin, hair, or eyes. Albinos have whitish hair, very pale or bright pink skin, and pink eyes. Some people have albino pets. Have you ever seen a white rabbit or mouse with pink eyes?

MINI-DATA

■ Hair and eye color

Children get their hair and eye color from their parents. Coloring from a mother and father can combine in a different way with each new baby.

▼ Hairs grow straight if the pits they grow from, called follicles, are round. If the follicles are flat, the hairs will grow out curly.

▲ Every child in a family carries his or her own mixture of the parents' looks. That's why some brothers and sisters look a lot alike, and others don't.

● **To the Parent**

Tracing family heritage in faces can be fun for children. It can also reinforce a sense of belonging. Some fascinating studies have been conducted that chart inherited ability, too—especially among artistic or musically gifted families. Children might try to identify shared tastes in hobbies, foods, or colors with other family members.

? Why Do Some People Talk Funny?

(ANSWER) Sometimes children are born with mouths shaped differently from most people. They might have trouble speaking. An operation can sometimes fix the problem. The children may also do exercises with their mouths and tongues until they learn to talk clearly. Other children may sound funny to you when they talk because they are just learning the language. Help them out!

■ It takes practice

Try to say "Moo!"

Meow?

Not quite! It's "Moo!"

Meoo?

Almost! Now try again: "Moo!"

Moo!

■ Foreign accents

When you grow up speaking one language, it's hard to learn to say all the words of another one correctly. If you know someone who speaks a foreign language, ask that person to teach you a few words. How do you sound?

Qvacque!

Quack!

● **To the Parent**

About 5,000 languages are spoken worldwide. Producing understandable speech in any one of them is a complicated process involving hearing, thought formulation, and control of mouth, throat, and breathing muscles. Encourage children to pronounce words correctly. Discourage making fun of a speech impediment or a foreign accent by explaining that it hurts feelings.

? Does Everyone Go to Church?

ANSWER Most people have a set of beliefs or a religion that helps them understand their lives. But each religion has its own way of doing things. People around the world have special ways of worshiping. Their religious buildings have many styles, too. Some people wear certain clothing because of their religion.

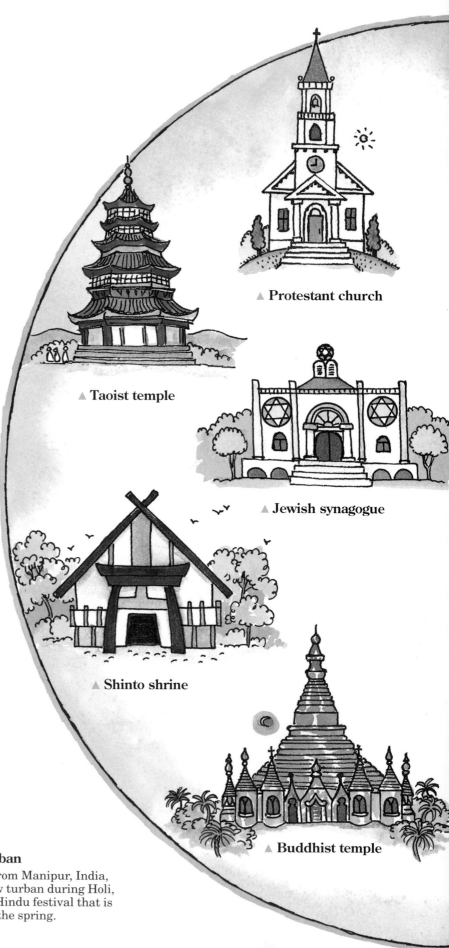

▲ Protestant church

▲ Taoist temple

▲ Jewish synagogue

▲ Shinto shrine

▲ Buddhist temple

◄ **A Hindu turban**
A young girl from Manipur, India, wears a yellow turban during Holi, a traditional Hindu festival that is celebrated in the spring.

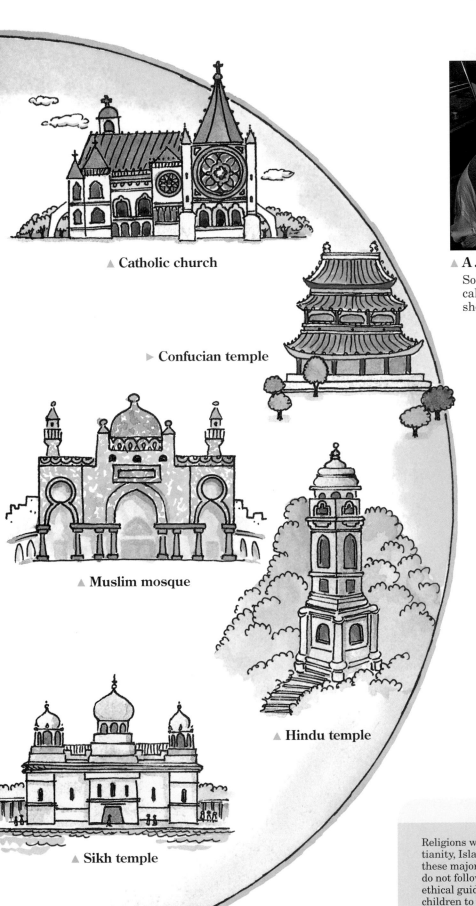

▲ Catholic church

▶ Confucian temple

▲ Muslim mosque

▲ Hindu temple

▲ Sikh temple

▲ **A Jewish yarmulke**

Some Jewish men and boys wear small caps called yarmulkes. They believe that the head should be covered during worship.

▲ **A Muslim chador**

Some Muslim women wear a chador—a veil that covers the face—whenever they go outside their own homes.

Why Are Some People Twins?

ANSWER Most human babies are born one at a time. But sometimes a mother has two or more babies at once. Two babies are called twins. Three are triplets. Four babies are quadruplets, and five at once—that's very rare!—are called quintuplets.

▼ **Identical twins**
Twins that look almost exactly alike are called identical twins. They are always the same sex, and they often have similar likes and dislikes.

▲ Fraternal twins

Fraternal twins are born at the same time, but they may not look alike. They can be the same or different sexes, and their personalities may be very different.

CHECK IT OUT

■ Twin destiny?

Studies show that identical twins share much more than looks. One set of twins who had been raised apart since birth met for the first time as adults. They found that they had both named their dogs "Toy." Also, they had both married women named Linda, worked the same kind of job, and vacationed on the same beach!

? Why Do People Get Scared?

ANSWER Things that you don't know much about can be scary. They can also frighten you when you remember something bad about them, like getting a shot at the doctor's office. It's common to be afraid of animals, insects, high places, the dark, or meeting new people. Usually when you get used to something, it no longer scares you.

◄ **Help! A monster!**
Objects in your room can look different—and scary—in the dark. A bad dream may include slightly different forms of your own familiar clothes and toys.

▲ Oops, sorry! Just a bathrobe!

If shadowy places frighten you at night, remember that they contain just everyday things. Turn on a light and get an adult to look for so-called "monsters" with you. See if you can pick out which item made which monster. Then you can all go back to sleep!

● **To the Parent**

Fear is a healthy response that evolved to protect humans from an environment full of strange and possibly harmful things. Fears originate in instinct, parental attitudes, and a child's own experience. Children's fears change as they mature and learn about the world; the best cures support that learning rather than belittle those fears. Introduce your children slowly and calmly to whatever scares them. The company of a confident child can encourage a timid one. Persistent or exaggerated fears may call for professional counseling.

Why Do People Argue?

Arguments often start when two people want different things. An argument can be short—about whose turn it is to do the dishes tonight, for example. Or it might continue for years, with one person trying to get another to agree, or to do what he wants. Most of the time, however, people can solve their differences without arguing.

■ A family feud

Families spend a lot of time together, so they may argue a lot. Kids often argue about sharing things such as toys, food, or their parents' attention. Parents may argue with kids about TV rules, bedtime, or homework.

I want pepperoni!

We had that last time! I want plain!

◄ I'll meet you halfway

When each person gives up a little, both people gain a lot. You can settle an argument by agreeing with the other person to do something that gives each one of you part of what you both want. That's called a compromise.

TRY THIS

■ Sorry about that, chief!

▼ Sometimes an argument isn't over until you apologize to the other person. This can be hard to do, but usually it works if you just say, "I'm sorry." You can add something about how you feel, like "I made a mistake" or "I hope we can be friends again." A heartfelt apology can work magic.

● To the Parent

Family therapists agree that a certain amount of arguing among siblings and parents is normal and healthy. Evidence shows that children even enjoy arguing, and that they use it to gain parental attention. If you feel there is too much fighting, try to analyze when it occurs. A quick before-dinner snack, for instance, can avert squabbles when kids are hungry or bored.

What Should I Do When I Get Mad?

(ANSWER) Getting angry is perfectly normal. It happens to everyone. You should let your parents and friends know about anything that's bothering you, but it's also important to show your anger in a way that helps you without hurting anyone else. Here are five suggestions. Can you think of some more?

■ Let's play "Tame the anger monster"!

Doing something physical is one of the best ways to get rid of anger. Working your muscles can cool off that hot, mad feeling. Or you can try using your anger to fix what caused it. Write down your problem, or—better yet—talk to an adult about it.

▶ **Write it out!**

◀ **Yell it out!**

◀ **Ride it out!**

▶ **Rip it out!**

▼ **Talk it out!**

● **To the Parent**

Teaching children appropriate ways to express their anger is a key parental and social responsibility. Moderate episodes of angry and aggressive behavior are a healthy part of development. Continual or excessive anger, however, may signal a need for special attention. Help your child work out anger by providing sympathy, cooling-off time, and vigorous activities.

How Can I Make New Friends?

ANSWER Have you ever felt lonely? Have you ever wanted to find a friend? Making friends doesn't happen by chance. You have to be friendly in order to make a friend. Try introducing yourself to another kid. You might say something like, "Hi, my name's ____! What's yours? What kind of games do you like to play?"

▼ **Say hello to someone new**
To gain a friend, you need to be a friend. You can start by saying "Hi" to someone new. Even dogs make new friends by acting friendly!

> Hi, my name's Rick! What's yours?

Nice shot!

▲ Pay a compliment

People like to get compliments. If you see someone doing a good job, tell him so.

▼ Lend a hand

You can make a new friend by offering help to someone who needs it. Don't you like someone who helps you out?

Want some help?

◀ Enjoy your friends!

By going out of their way to be friendly, these children have become good friends. Now they can have a great time playing together.

● To the Parent

Friends are important to young children, especially from age five up. Companions can help develop social skills and raise self-esteem. You can assist a shy child by encouraging social situations. Be patient, though: It takes years for children to learn the skills of sharing and compromise that go into a mature friendship.

Why Is Honesty the Best Policy?

ANSWER Sometimes it is hard to tell the truth. After all, if you've done something wrong, you don't want to get in trouble. But telling a lie can make things worse. It makes you feel bad, and it doesn't solve the problem. If you tell the truth, you can fix the problem—and feel better—right away.

▶ Taylor was running in his house when he knocked over a lamp and broke it. Nobody saw him do it. When his mother asked him how the lamp got broken, Taylor was afraid to tell her. So he lied and said he didn't know.

▼ Taylor's mom asked everyone what had happened to the lamp. He felt guilty as he watched her. Taylor wondered what he should do.

Taylor started feeling so bad that he ran to his mother and told her the truth: "Mom, I broke the lamp by accident. I'm sorry. I'll be more careful next time." His mother understood. She suggested they fix the lamp together. Taylor felt so good about being honest that his smile shone brighter than the lamp!

❓ Why Did I Get Picked Last?

ANSWER When kids get picked for a team, somebody has to be the last one chosen. If you have ever been that "somebody," you probably got your feelings hurt. Just remember that no one can be good at everything. A kid who is good at basketball might be lousy at swimming or music.

■ What am I good at?

If you don't get chosen for a team, you will feel better by remembering all the things you are good at. What kinds of activities do you like most? Do you enjoy thinking games more than sports?

◄ You may like playing a musical instrument or acting in a play. If so, you could join a band or a drama group rather than a sports team.

▲ You may not be tall enough for basketball, but you might have a talent for skating or other sports, such as skating or hiking.

■ Shoot and shoot again

The best way to master something is to practice. Practice may not make you perfect, but it sure will make you better! All the best players had to practice a lot in order to get as good as they are.

▼ Maybe you're good at playing chess. If you enjoy something, ask your friends to join you. Don't wait for them to ask you!

▲ **She never gave up**

When swimmer Amy Van Dyken was a child, her classmates teased her and picked her last for teams. But Amy was determined, and she worked hard. As a result, she won four gold medals at the 1996 Olympics.

● **To the Parent**

Because they lack an adult's perspective, children are especially hurt by rejection. When your child feels rejected, remind him that he cannot excel at everything, and help him remember his strengths. Encourage your child to take up activities in which he feels competent. Competence breeds confidence, which in turn makes it easier to bounce back from rejection.

Why Is It Important to Keep a Promise?

ANSWER When someone makes a promise to you, you expect her to keep it, and you are disappointed if she does not. When you make a promise, you are asking someone to trust you. And when you follow through on a promise, people know they can rely on you. This will earn you lasting friendships.

◄ Andrew promised his little brother that he would come home after school to help him build a model plane. Later that day, however, some of Andrew's friends asked him to go swimming at the same time.

Always
Keep Your
Promises!

► Andrew remembered his promise. He told his friends that he wished he could go swimming with them, but that he had promised to help his brother at 3:00.

54

On the way home, Andrew thought about the fun he was missing. He wished he had gone with his friends.

At home, Andrew's brother was waiting for him. He had been looking forward to working on the model all day. Andrew felt good that he had made his little brother so happy.

Andrew and his brother had a great time making the plane together. Now Andrew was glad that he had kept his promise. "Besides," he thought, "I can always go swimming another day."

● To the Parent

Keeping one's word does not come naturally to small children because of the time lag between saying and doing. You can help your child learn by example. Try to keep your promises whenever possible. If you have to change your plans, explain it to her and acknowledge her disappointment. When she keeps her word, praise her and let her know that her actions are important.

Why Can't I Always Do What My Friends Are Doing?

ANSWER Sometimes your parents won't let you do something that your friends want you to do. That's not because your mom and dad are uncool or out of touch. It's because they think you may be too young for that activity, or because they know it isn't safe. Try to make sure you understand their reasons.

▶ **You never let me do anything...**
Imagine that some friends have invited you to go fishing where it isn't allowed. Your parents know the dock is unsafe, so they say you can't go along.

▼ **...and now I know why!**
Even though the friends know that fishing is not allowed, they go anyway. Now they've got big trouble on their hands!

What If a "Friend" Wants Me to Do Something Wrong?

A friend may ask you to join her in doing something that you know is wrong. You don't have to agree just to be nice. Think for yourself. Tell her firmly that you can't join her.

Come up with another activity that you could both do instead. If in doubt, you can suggest that you both ask your parents.

▲ **Find a better game**
The foolish monkey wants to climb a dangerous electrified fence. What a stupid stunt! The smart one looks for a safer sport, such as climbing a tree.

● **To the Parent**

Children need guidance in developing sound judgment about what they should and should not do. Help your child by setting clear expectations. Be able to answer her questions about why certain activities are not allowed. Above all, be consistent. If peer pressure is involved, help your child practice saying "no" to her friends.

Why Is It Important to Think of Others?

ANSWER Think how sad your life would be if no one was nice to you. How would you feel if no one ever helped you out? Luckily, the world is not like that. You can do your part by helping other people. It will make them feel good, and it will make you feel happy.

▲ **In the kitchen: Pitch in!**
Your aid can mean a lot to your family. You can help your mom or dad make dinner by picking out lettuce at the grocery store. At home, you can mix the salad.

▶ **Dish it out**
Your parents will love it if you work with them to set the dining table or serve the food. Walk slowly so you don't spill anything!

► Lend a drying hand

Your mom or dad may be tired after a long day at work. Wouldn't it be nice to help them out by drying the pots and pans and putting away the dishes?

▲ Offer to take out the trash

Without being asked or reminded to, try taking out the trash when it is full. Tie the bag tightly so nothing spills out, then put it carefully in the garbage can.

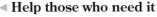

◄ Help those who need it

If a relative or a friend of the family is sick or unable to cook for herself, your family can share a hot meal with her. Think how glad she will feel to know that you thought of her and wanted to help!

● To the Parent

Empathy—the ability to think of others—does not come easily to small children, who learn it only gradually. You can help your child develop a sense of empathy by telling him how much his aid means and thanking him whenever he is helpful. Being cheerful and appreciative goes a long way toward making the act of helping fun.

What Is "Playing Fair"?

ANSWER You are playing fair when you follow the rules of a game and don't try to bend or break them. You may feel upset if you lose, but you can be proud that you played honestly. No one likes to play with a cheater. Remember that cheaters are really just cheating themselves. They can't feel proud of winning if they didn't win fair and square.

▼ **Your cheatin' hearts**
This sneaky dog is cheating in a game of cards. When the other players find out, they will be angry.

▲ Who feels worse?

This girl ruined a fun game of soccer when she made her friend fall down. Do you think she felt bad afterward?

◄ Be a good sport

One of these tennis players won a match against the other, but it's hard to tell who's who because they're both happy that they played well. Good sports smile and shake hands after a game, even when they lose.

Why Is It Bad to Snoop?

ANSWER If you are curious and want to find out something, the best way is to ask about it openly. Never snoop behind someone's back. Why? Because snooping is sneaky, and people will get angry if you pry into their private lives. Besides, you never know if snooping will spoil a nice surprise!

◄ When the phone rings and the call is for someone else, you may be tempted to listen in on the conversation. If you are asked not to listen, the person might have a very good reason. So be considerate: Don't eavesdrop on other people's conversations.

Surprise!!

▼ If you listen, you may hear something you were not supposed to. Now your surprise party won't be a surprise!

Why Is It Mean to Whisper?

When you whisper about someone in front of that person, he may imagine the worst. Even if you are saying nice things about him, he may think that you are making fun of him instead. That's why whispers can hurt feelings.

▲ When the kids at left whisper that they like their friend's new haircut, the friend feels bad because he cannot hear what they are saying. He thinks he must look silly, or mean, or dumb.

■ Don't be a spy

This girl made her brother angry and embarrassed by snooping through his things. Don't go through someone else's belongings unless you have permission.

● To the Parent

Children are naturally inquisitive, but they need to learn the limits of curiosity. Let your child ask questions, but encourage him to respect the privacy and wishes of others. If a child has been snooping, discuss how he would feel if someone did it to him. Help him define the places in your house that are off-limits.

Is It All Right to Cry?

ANSWER When something makes you very sad, your feelings might confuse you. You may want to cry all the time, or not at all. You may get more tired than you normally do. You may even get angry about what happened. All of these feelings are normal, and you don't have to hold them in.

■ About feeling sad

Sadness is not always a bad thing. When you go off by yourself to cry, you are giving your mind and your body time to think, rest, and feel better after sudden changes. Crying can also be a sign to others that you need extra TLC (tender loving care). Most of us feel much better after we've had a good cry.

■ Ways to cope with grief

Sadness is tiring, so get plenty of rest and eat healthy food when you are feeling sad. You don't have to act sad all the time, either: If you feel mad inside, pound it out! If you feel like playing or kidding around, do so. And try to remember that sooner or later things will get better. Grief goes away after a while.

■ Focus on the good times

If you have lost a pet or a relative, you can help yourself heal by remembering the good times you had. If your dog has died, think of all the fun things you liked to do together: playing in the park, going for walks, sharing kisses. It's fine to remember the bad things, too—like that time he chewed up your toys!

● To the Parent

Allowing children to show grief helps them work through their feelings. Parents may see significant changes in sleep, eating, and behavioral patterns. Many normally sociable children like to be alone for a while when they are upset. It's best to respect a child's sadness but be prepared to offer comfort, distraction, or a favorite activity if the grief seems excessive.

How Can I Help If Something Bad Happens to a Friend?

ANSWER When something bad happens to a friend—an illness or a death in the family, perhaps—you can be a big help to that person simply by acting like a friend. People in trouble aren't suddenly different. Your friends are still themselves even when they are unhappy.

◀ Don't avoid a friend who is sad
You may feel shy about talking to someone who is glum or crying. But saying right away that you are sorry about what's happening to them can make both of you feel better. It may even make your friendship stronger.

▶ Don't take it personally
Some people prefer to be left alone when they are unhappy, so don't feel hurt if your friend ignores you or brushes you off. It's his own feelings—not you—that he doesn't like.

■ How else can I cheer him up?

▲ Split a pizza

▲ Offer homemade treats

▲ Send a card

▲ Ask him over to play

▲ Draw pictures together

▲ Ride bikes

▲ Call up just to say "Hi!"

▲ Share a funny story

● **To the Parent**

Children often want to help when tragedy strikes someone they know, but they will probably need assistance from you. You can suggest that they offer flowers or a homemade gift or card; take over chores like walking the dog; or act as a homework messenger if missed days of school are involved. Remind children to give their friends time—and not to expect too much grateful response.

Is It Ever Okay to Be a Tattletale?

ANSWER When someone else is doing something wrong or breaking a rule, it doesn't always help for you to tell on them. Try to fix the problem yourself first without going to an adult. Remember that most people, including parents, soon stop listening to tattletales.

▶ **What happens to tattletales?**
Other kids might decide you're not much fun to play with if you always tattle about unimportant things. They won't want to be around you if you keep getting them in trouble.

When Is It Good to Tell?

It's very important to tell an adult if you think someone is in danger. If you see someone doing something dangerous, and that person doesn't stop when you warn him, tell an adult right away. If you see someone hurting another person—even by accident—go tell an adult. That way the injured person can be helped quickly, if need be.

Real rewards

Being a tattletale when safety is involved is being the right kind of tattletale. We all like to play with friends who care about us.

What's Wrong with Bragging?

(ANSWER) Everyone has a right to be proud of doing things well. But if you brag too much about how good you are, you're not giving others a chance to share the things that they are good at. Soon they will get tired of hearing so much about you (just as you would get tired of hearing so much about them). When that happens, no one has a good time.

Bragging can make others feel bad. Showing off your expensive shoes or good grades does not make you a more likable person.

■ If you're an ace at something...

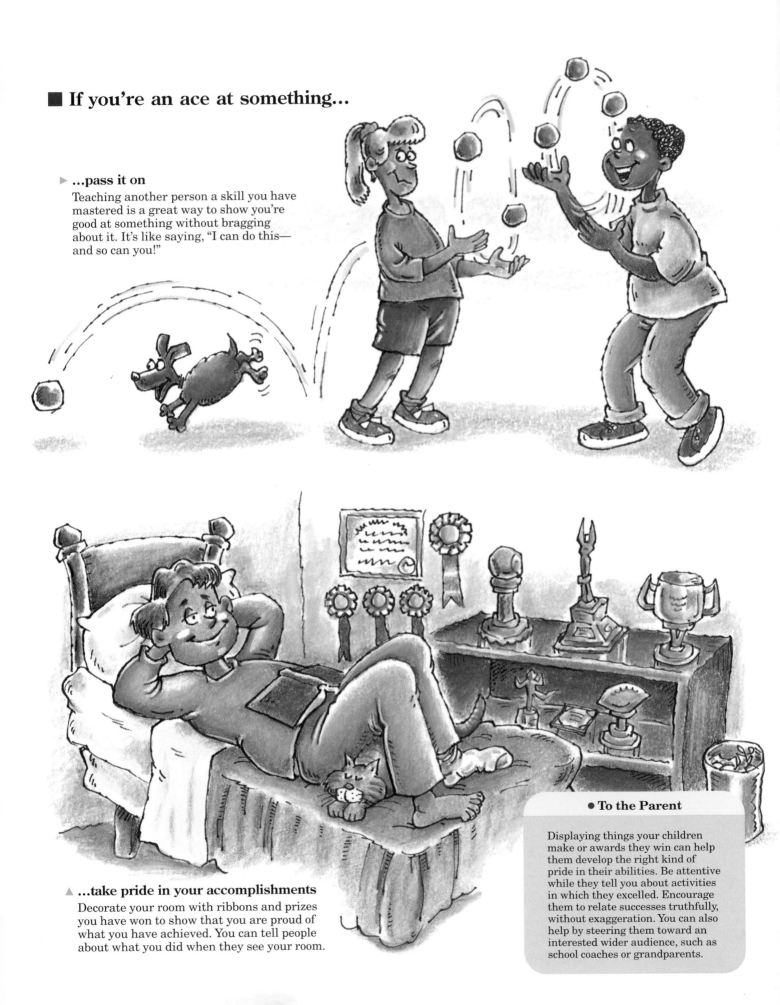

▶ **...pass it on**
Teaching another person a skill you have mastered is a great way to show you're good at something without bragging about it. It's like saying, "I can do this—and so can you!"

▲ **...take pride in your accomplishments**
Decorate your room with ribbons and prizes you have won to show that you are proud of what you have achieved. You can tell people about what you did when they see your room.

● To the Parent

Displaying things your children make or awards they win can help them develop the right kind of pride in their abilities. Be attentive while they tell you about activities in which they excelled. Encourage them to relate successes truthfully, without exaggeration. You can also help by steering them toward an interested wider audience, such as school coaches or grandparents.

❓ What Is Loyalty?

ANSWER Loyalty means standing by your friend, your team, or your family, even if you don't feel like it. When you are loyal to a friend, you help her when she's in trouble and defend her if people are picking on her. Loyalty lets people trust and depend on one another.

■ Loyalty to your family

▲ Loyalty to your family can be hard. You may not want to protect your kid brother at school when other kids are making fun of him. You know they might make fun of you, too.

◄ But if you don't stand up for your brother, who will? If you are loyal to your family, they will be loyal to you. Being able to depend on your family is a good feeling.

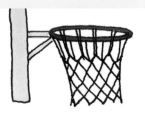

■ Loyalty to a team

Loyalty to your team means being reliable. It means coming to all the practices and doing your best during games. If you don't, you're letting down not just your team, but yourself.

■ Can loyalty go too far?

▼ Should you be loyal to a friend who asks you to do something wrong? No, loyalty doesn't mean covering for someone who's stealing or lying. If someone asks you to do that, she's not a true friend.

● **To the Parent**

Loyalty can be confusing. Some children may expect other kids to cover for them when they do something wrong. You can explain to children that there's a difference between tattling and being honest. Let them understand that true friendship does not include helping others get away with things they shouldn't do.

? What Can I Do If People Make Fun of Me?

ANSWER Some people feel important only when they are making fun of other people. They might hurt your feelings on purpose just to get a laugh from other kids. They may tease you to cover up their own feeling of weakness. Here are some ways to deal with the situation.

Hey, Four Eyes!

◄ Ignore it

The person teasing you wants to see you get upset. If you pretend he's not bothering you, he might lose interest.

▼ Talk to an adult

It's best to try to solve problems with a bully yourself. But sometimes nothing works. If you get to this point, don't be embarrassed to talk to a teacher or a parent.

▲ Respond with humor

A bully usually isn't prepared for a comeback. Try using humor to stop him cold. For example, if someone calls you "Four Eyes," just say, "That's why I can see twice as well as you!"

● To the Parent

If your child is being teased, advise him either to ignore or to talk to the bully first. Help him understand that bullies are often motivated by their own insecurity. If the teasing seems to go too far or becomes physical, you may need to step in and solve the problem with the other child's parents or teacher.

Do People Turn Green with Envy?

ANSWER No, not really. Envy is that grumpy feeling you get when you want something that someone else has. Some people say that envy makes you feel sick. When you feel sick, your face is pale or even greenish, so that's why people sometimes say they "turn green with envy."

■ Envy hurts a friend

It's okay to admire a friend's new bike. But when you get mad at him for having something you don't, that's envy. Don't give in to that feeling. You might hurt your friend's feelings or even ruin your friendship.

■ Turning green, feeling blue

Envy can make you mad. It can also make you sad. People sometimes feel sorry for themselves because they don't have the things they want. But it's important to be thankful for the things you *do* have.

■ The "green-eyed monster"

Writer William Shakespeare described envy as a "green-eyed monster." He said the monster would gobble up people who were envious! That was his way of saying that envious people would hurt only themselves.

■ A way around the problem

One way to stop envy is to share. If you get a new bike, remember that your friends may be jealous, so let them try it out, too. That way, everyone will get a chance to ride it.

● To the Parent

The Greek poet Sappho first used "green" to describe envy in the seventh century B.C. The Greeks believed that envy made the body produce too much bile, causing a person's face to turn pale or greenish. The poets Ovid and Chaucer also used the color green to denote envy long before Shakespeare's famous description of it in *Othello*.

Why Do I Have to Be Nice to My Kid Sister or Brother?

 ANSWER Little brothers and sisters can be pests. They want to do everything you do. Sometimes you just want to do things by yourself without them tagging along. But try to see it from their point of view. They love you. They probably think your life is more exciting than theirs. They can be your loyal friends and playmates.

▼ You may think of your kid brother as a ball and chain, but to him you're a superhero! He looks up to you because you're older and can do things that he can't.

■ Goodnight, Chet!

The age advantage
You might get to stay up when your kid brother goes to bed. You'll be home without a sitter when he still needs one. And you'll get to drive first.

■ Making a "new" friend

◄ You might find that your brother's not so bad after all. He could bait your hook for you when you go fishing. Or you could teach him to play games with you when your parents are too busy.

● To the Parent

It's important to encourage older siblings to involve younger ones in some of their activities. But be sensitive to the fact that an older sibling needs time to herself, too. Spend more time, if you can, with an older child who wants time alone with a parent. This will give the child a break from acting as a parent to the younger sibling.

How Can I Help Make the World a Better Place?

ANSWER Making the whole world better sounds impossible. But it's not as hard as you think. There are all sorts of small things you can do right where you live. Why bother?

Because if you help improve the world, you, your family and friends, and people everywhere will have a better place to live!

◄ **At school**

You could help a classmate with her science project. Then she could help you with your math homework.

▼ **At play**

Invite someone new to join your team. You could wind up with a new friend—and a much better team!

▼ **Around town**

Volunteer for a community project, like picking up trash at your local park. Offer to rake leaves for a neighbor who no longer can.

Growing-Up Album

Spot the Twins 82
Who's Missing Manners? 84
What Would You Do If...? 86

Spot the Twins

Nine sets of twins went to see the county fair.
But when each one turned around, his partner wasn't
there! Can you help them find each other? Here's a clue
for you: Things, not just people, can travel two by two!

82

Answers: Twin teddy bears; twin girls with hats and red sweaters; twin girls with ponytails; twin ducks; twin boys with striped shirts; twin balloons; twin clowns; twin men with mustaches; twin dogs.

Who's Missing Manners?

Good manners can help you in all kinds of situations, including the ones shown here. Which characters are doing the right thing? Which others need reminding?

Right: Raccoon using chopsticks; cat using fork and knife. Boy wiping nose with handkerchief; girl covering mouth to yawn. Two boys in sandbox asking third boy to play.

Wrong: Wolf talking with his mouth full; pig eating with his hands. Boy sneezing all over the place. Boy not taking turns; girl not sharing toys. Boy kicking and pulling shirt of other player; boy touching soccer ball with hands.

What Would You Do If...?

Now that you know good manners make people feel better, put your knowledge into action! You can start by taking the fun quiz below. In each scene, ask yourself this question: What you would do if...

...you were behind someone carrying a bunch of packages into a building?

a. Steal one of the packages; the person won't notice.
b. Make fun of the person by imitating how he is walking.
c. Say, "Let me help you," then hold the door open for him.

...someone sent you a present?

a. Give it to your baby sister; it's fun to watch her break stuff!
b. Cry out in a disappointed voice, "*This* isn't what I wanted!"
c. Write a thank-you note to the sender.

...a new kid moved in next door?

a. Make up some scary stories about a neighborhood gang.
b. Ignore him—you have plenty of friends already.
c . Ask him what kinds of games he likes to play.

...toys were scattered all around when it was time to leave a friend's house?

a. Refuse to come back until the room is clean.
b. Ask your friend, "Don't you have an au pair?"
c. Help your friend pick up all the toys before you leave.

...a "friend" said, "Let's steal some candy!"

a. Do what she says, so you won't lose a "friend."
b. Reply, "I'll bet I can steal more candy than you can!"
c. Say, "That's a dumb idea," then find a new friend.

...you accidentally broke a toy that belonged to someone else?

a. Tell the owner, "A Martian landed and broke your toy!"
b. Pretend you weren't there when it happened.
c. Apologize for your mistake, then offer to replace the toy.

 0-5 points: Please read the book again!

 5½ points: You are almost a model citizen!

 6 points: You earn the 1st Prize Ribbon!

Scoring: Give yourself 0 points for each "a" answer, ½ point for each "b," and 1 point for each "c."

TIME®
LIFE
BOOKS

Time-Life Books is a division of Time Life Inc.

TIME LIFE INC.

PRESIDENT and CEO: George Artandi

TIME-LIFE BOOKS

PRESIDENT: John D. Hall
PUBLISHER/MANAGING EDITOR: Neil Kagan

A Child's First Library of Learning
FEELINGS & MANNERS

EDITORS: Karin Kinney, Allan Fallow
DIRECTOR, NEW PRODUCT DEVELOPMENT: Elizabeth D. Ward
MARKETING DIRECTOR: Janine Wilkin

Deputy Editor: Terrell Smith
Picture Coordinator: David A. Herod
Picture Researcher: Mary M. Saxton

Design: Studio A—Antonio Alcalá, Virginia Ibarra-Garza,
Wendy Schleicher, Melissa Wilets
Special Contributors: Vilasini Balakrishnan, Kristen Desmond,
Andrew Gutelle, Jocelyn Lindsay, Barry Wolverton (research and
writing); Colette Stockum (copyedit).

Consultant: Thomas J. Cottle, a sociologist and practicing clinical
psychologist, has taught at Harvard, Wesleyan University, and Amherst
College. His books include *The Voices of School* and *Time's Children.*

Correspondents: Maria Vincenza Aloisi (Paris), Christine Hinze
(London), Christina Lieberman (New York).

Vice President, Director of Finance: Christopher Hearing
Vice President, Book Production: Marjann Caldwell
Director of Photography and Research: John Conrad Weiser
Director of Editorial Administration: Barbara Levitt
Production Manager: Marlene Zack
Quality Assurance Manager: Dominique Fleurima
Library: Louise D. Forstall

Photography: Cover: ©Richard Hutchings/Photo Researchers.
Back Cover: JoAnn Simmons-Swing. 1: © Roy Morsch/The Stock Mar-
ket. 28: © Paul Avis/Gamma Liaison. 34: © Tom McCarthy/The Stock
Market. 35: © Rhoda Sidney/PhotoEdit. 38: (c) Jehangir Gazdar/Wood-
fin Camp & Associates. 39: © J. Polleross/The Stock Market (top);
© Alain Evrard/Photo Researchers (bottom). 40: © DiMaggio/Kalish/
The Stock Market. 41: © Roy Morsch/The Stock Market. 53: AP/Wide
World Photos. 81: © Tony Freeman/PhotoEdit.

Illustrations: **Loel Barr:** 4-5, 8 *(top right),* 9, 17 *(bottom left),* 26 *(top
right),* 27, 28, 30, 31 *(bottom),* 42-43, 52-53, 61, 70-71, 74-75. **Leila Cabib:**
17 *(top right and middle),* 40-41, 50-51, 66-67, 80. **Yvonne Gensurowsky:**
26 *(bottom).* **Linda Greigg:** 29, 58-59. **Annie Lunsford:** 6, 8 *(bottom),*
20-21, 22, 36-37, 56-57, 60, 68-69. **Roz Schanzer:** 10-11, 14-15, 18-19, 32-33,
38-39, 48-49, 62-63, 72-73, 76-77, 82-87. **Bethann Thornburgh:** 7, 12-13,
16, 23, 24-25, 31 *(top right and middle),* 35, 44-45, 46-47, 54-55, 64-65, 78-
79. **Stephen Wagner:** front and back cover illustrations.

First printing. Printed in U.S.A.
Published simultaneously in Canada.
School and library distribution by Time-Life Education, P.O. Box 85026,
Richmond, Virginia 23285-5026.

Time Life is a trademark of Time Warner Inc. U.S.A.

Library of Congress Cataloging in Publication Data
Feelings & Manners.
    88 pp.   1.4 cm.—(A child's first library of learning)
    Summary: Explains why there are rules for behavior and examines
common feelings and values by answering such questions as: "Why do I
have to share my toys?", "Why do people argue?", and "What is playing
fair?".
    ISBN 0-8094-9483-3
    1. Socialization—Juvenile literature. 2. Social skills—Juvenile litera-
ture. [1. Socialization—Miscellanea. 2. Conduct of life—Miscellanea.
3. Questions and answers.] I. Time-Life Books. II. Series.
HQ783.F437   1997
303.3'2—DC21   96-40922
                                                              CIP
                                                              AC Rev

OTHER PUBLICATIONS:

COOKING	DO IT YOURSELF
Weight Watchers® Smart Choice Recipe Collection	The Time-Life Complete Gardener
	Home Repair and Improvement
Great Taste–Low Fat	The Art of Woodworking
Williams-Sonoma Kitchen Library	Fix It Yourself

TIME-LIFE KIDS	HISTORY
Family Time Bible Stories	The American Story
Library of First Questions and Answers	Voices of the Civil War
A Child's First Library of Learning	The American Indians
I Love Math	Lost Civilizations
Nature Company Discoveries	Mysteries of the Unknown
Understanding Science & Nature	Time Frame
	The Civil War
SCIENCE/NATURE	Cultural Atlas
Voyage Through the Universe	

For information on and a full description of any of the Time-Life Books
series listed above, please call 1-800-621-7026 or write:

Reader Information
Time-Life Customer Service
P.O. Box C-32068
Richmond, Virginia 23261-2068